ANOINTED
for Mission

Exercising Your Baptismal Call

STEPHEN S. WILBRICHT, csc

Nihil Obstat
Deacon Daniel G. Welter, JD
Chancellor
Archdiocese of Chicago
May 24, 2022

Imprimatur
Most Rev. Robert G. Casey
Vicar General
Archdiocese of Chicago
May 24, 2022

ANOINTED FOR MISSION: EXERCISING YOUR BAPTISMAL CALL © 2022 Archdiocese of Chicago: Liturgy Training Publications, 3949 South Racine Avenue, Chicago, IL 60609; 800-933-1800; fax: 800-933-7094; email: orders@ltp.org; website: www.LTP.org. All rights reserved.

This book was edited by Mary G. Fox. Víctor R. Pérez was the production editor, Anna Manhart was the designer, and Juan Alberto Castillo was the production artist.

Cover and interior art by James B. Janknegt.

26 25 24 23 22   1 2 3 4 5

Printed in the United States of America

Library of Congress Control Number: 2022941344

ISBN: 978-1-61671-685-1

AFM

CONTENTS

✤

INTRODUCTION

❖

A visitor to any parish during the week will see parishioners contributing to the life of the community in myriad ways. Some will be teaching adults or children, others will be planning the parish budget, organizing activities for the youth group, gardening, gathering church linens to be washed, distributing canned goods at the food pantry, or coordinating liturgical ministers. All these members of the faith community are exercising their baptismal call and, in doing so, are living as disciples.

This book will help parishioners become more grounded in the communal nature of baptism and in how they are called to live out their discipleship. As baptism incorporates new Christians into life in the Body of Christ, it makes them sharers in a royal priesthood, in a mission to preach the Gospel to draw others to belief in Christ. Through baptism, they are one with other disciples who daily die to self to rise in Christ.

For parishioners to come to a deeper understanding of baptism, leaders of organizations, teams, or groups in the parish—from teams of catechists to the pastoral council to gardeners—will want to make reflecting on this book a part of their meetings. Heads of groups may invite their members to read the short chapters prior to meetings and to discuss the questions at the end of the chapter during the first fifteen minutes of their meeting. If a group reflects together on this book monthly, by the end of the year, their deeper understanding of baptism will be reflected by the unity they seek, the hospitality they show, and their work in building up the Body of Christ.

The first part of this book explores the meaning of baptism and how it is lived. Chapter 1 presents baptism as the sacrament of discipleship, the primary way in which people respond to the call to follow Christ. Chapter 2 examines how a parish might look different if parishioners discerned their gifts. In other words, how might men and women be called forth prayerfully to use their gifts for the building up of Christ's Body? Chapter 3 proposes how baptism might be a ticket for renewal and transformation of parish life, offering biblical images that demonstrate that all leadership is servant oriented. Part 2 of the book provides seven traditional descriptions of baptism that are the source for reflection and prayer. Questions that follow the reflections will prompt discussion on how the parish lives out these aspects of baptism. May this short consideration of our common baptism help renew in us the spirit of baptismal discipleship, for from the greatest to the least, all are called not "to be served but to serve" (Matthew 20:28).

WHOLE PARISH FORMATION

Your parish may want to offer formation that may be adapted for small groups or the entire faith community to explore the meaning of their baptism. A five-week series outline, with suggestions for prayer and discussion, and links to videos on our baptismal calling, is available at the website LTP.org/Anointed.

PART 1

THE COMMUNAL NATURE OF BAPTISM

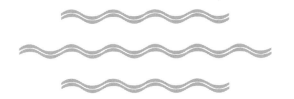

CHAPTER 1

Baptism as the Foundation of the Church

Almighty God, the Father of our Lord Jesus Christ,
has freed you from sin,
given you new birth by water and the Holy Spirit,
and joined you to his people.
He now anoints you with the Chrism of salvation,
So that you may remain as a member of Christ, Priest,
Prophet and King, unto eternal life.

—*Order of Baptism of Children*, 98

As the minister of baptism anoints the forehead with the oil of chrism immediately after a child is immersed in water, the prayer being uttered manifests what takes place at the font. The child is bestowed "new birth by water and the Holy Spirit." The immersion into the waters of baptism has freed the child from all sin and gives entrance into the Church. However, perhaps the most important part of this prayer is the commissioning for the child to live forever as a *member* of Christ's Body, sharing in his mission as "Priest, Prophet and King."

Baptism means discipleship! For far too long, baptism has been minimized in the Christian imagination to simply be the sacramental gift that guarantees a share in "eternal life." Thus, baptism became equated with insurance. With it, Christians could be assured of a much easier time gaining the prize of heaven. Missing in this understanding of the sacrament is the Christian mission itself: the willingness to preach the Gospel in word and in action to draw others to belief in Christ and hope for the dawning of God's reign on earth. Discipleship demands the daily discovery of precisely what it means to be anointed "Priest, Prophet and King" for Christ's mission today.

What would happen if we could recapture the communal nature of baptism, if we could rid believers of the false notion that baptism is solely for the individual rather than for the Church? Those who enter the font, whether they be newborn infants or mature adults, embark on a new way of life, life with Christ. This life gives the newly baptized an entirely new set of relationships—namely, the bonds of unity that are meant to be forged among all the baptized. In this sense, one is not immersed alone in the waters of baptism; one is plunged into the very life that unites Christians of all time, living and dead. It is simply impossible to celebrate the sacrament of baptism privately, just as it is impossible to live out the Christian life privately.

Yet a privatized setting for the celebration of baptism became common, while the understanding of the sacrament would shift from discipleship to the pledge of eternal life for the newly baptized. What would mark this shift is the gradual demise of adult baptism, calling for a mature commitment to Christianity, as well as the rise of infant baptism, seen as necessary for the rejection of sin and the planting of the seeds of faith. Consequently, baptism quickly came to be interpreted as a once-in-a-lifetime moment at which a child is born as a new creation, worthy of God's love and care. What has been lost is the notion that baptism is a daily event in which men and women make a conscious decision to die to self to live for others in Christ. Attitudes toward baptism may liken the sacrament to a commodity that is easily purchased, with little sacrifice, quickly forgotten, and put on the shelf.

Nevertheless, much has been done since the Second Vatican Council to restore the understanding of baptism as the primary sacrament for discipleship. With great effort, theologians, bishops, and pastors have underscored baptism as a sacrament that concerns and unites all Christians on a common pilgrim journey toward salvation with God. The Second Vatican Council stirred up a baptismal consciousness, which is based on the importance of all the baptized playing a role in the building up of the Body of Christ and in the sharing of Christ's message to heal the brokenhearted. Scattered throughout the council's sixteen primary constitutions and decrees are images of the Church that reveal its baptismal character. For example, the opening words of *Lumen gentium (LG),* the Council's *Dogmatic Constitution on the Church*, refers to the Church as a "sacrament" of unity among disciples. It is to be a visible manifestation of God's grace:

> Since the church, in Christ, is a sacrament—a sign and instrument, that is, of communion with God and of the unity of the entire human race—it here proposes, for the benefit of the faithful and of the entire world, to describe more clearly, and in the tradition laid down by earlier council, its own nature and universal mission.[1]

Unity, or communion, is precisely the sacramental nature of the Church, or what the Church is called to make visibly present to the world. The apostle Paul preached extensively using the "Body of Christ" as a primary image of the Church. Just as the parts of the human body are both numerous and diverse, so too are the many members of the Body of Christ (1 Corinthians 12:12). *Lumen gentium* elaborates on this theme of the Church as a unified body:

---

1. *Lumen gentium* (LG), 1.

In this body the life of Christ is communicated to those who believe and who, through the sacraments, are united in a hidden and real way to Christ in his passion and glorification. Through Baptism we are formed in the likeness of Christ: "For in one Spirit we were all baptized into one body" (1 Corinthians 12:13). In this sacred rite our union with Christ's death and resurrection is symbolized and effected: "For we were buried with him by Baptism into death"; and if "we have been united with him in the likeness of his death, we shall be so in the likeness of his resurrection also" (Romans 6:4–5).[2]

Continuing, this paragraph emphasizes the important role that diversity plays within the body. Unity is not achieved through uniformity or the demand that every part of the body function in the same way. Instead, unity is based upon an appreciation of the unique contribution that each member makes for the good of the whole:

A diversity of members and functions is engaged in the building up of Christ's body, too. There is only one Spirit who, out of his own richness and the needs of the ministries, gives his various gifts for the welfare of the church (see 1 Corinthians 12:1–11). . . . The same Spirit who of himself is the principle of unity in the body, by his own power and by the interior cohesion of the members produces and stimulates love among the faithful. From this it follows that if one member suffers in any way, all the members suffer, and if one member is honored, all the members together rejoice (see 1 Corinthians 12:26).[3]

In a similar way, Paul instructs the Galatians on the equality of membership in the Body of Christ: "There is neither Jew nor Greek, there is neither slave nor free person, there is not male and female; for you all are one in Christ Jesus" (Galatians 3:28). Baptism bestows a oneness among members that cannot be separated by human

2. LG, 7.

3. LG, 7.

categories of judgment and perception. This means that even though my eyes can detect a difference in gender, no such distinction serves to separate the parts of Christ's Body. Christians do not stand out within the Body as individuals, but rather, they stand together as an inherently interconnected whole. As one theologian writes: "The emphasis in not on the role of Christians taken as individuals but rather as members of the body of Christ. The faithful find their dignity rooted in the gift of baptism through which even as lay persons they share in the priestly and prophetic office of Christ."[4]

Christian baptism is all about discipleship, and discipleship in turn is all about mission. Although the three-fold office of Christ, and our participation in it, will be a theme running throughout this book, it is important to summarize the meaning of this baptis-

Christian baptism is all about discipleship, and discipleship in turn is all about mission.

mal anointing. Three questions need to be asked: What is a priest? What is a prophet? What is a king? A priest is someone who makes a sacrifice. A prophet is someone who challenges others to see the truth. A king is someone who rules, and in the case of Christ, ruling is all about servant leadership. Therefore, the sacrament of baptism informs newly made Christians of their dignity and their responsibility of sharing in the life and mission of Christ: a way of total selflessness in charity, witness, and leadership.

Baptism makes priests out of all Christians, while some are called by God to be anointed as presbyters to serve and order the baptismal priesthood. Christians exercise a priestly, prophetic, and royal ministry not only through their participation in the Eucharist, but in their contributions to the workplace, the family, and the simple tasks of everyday life. During the COVID-19 pandemic,

4. Michael A. Fahey, "Church," in *Systematic Theology: Roman Catholic Perspectives*, vol. 2, ed. Francis Schüssler Fiorenza and John Galvin (Minneapolis, MN: Fortress Press, 1991), 44.

Christians unable to assemble in public found other ways of nurturing the Christian spirit. They discovered satisfaction in simple acts of charity and quiet outreach, and communal connection in new forms of prayer and devotion. Able to assemble once more, we must continue to examine our call to be disciples. Both liturgical and ecclesial ministries must be strengthened, so that all members of the Body of Christ are able to live out their vocation as disciples of Christ, sharing in his office as priest, prophet, and king.

❖ Discussion Questions ❖

1. What is your personal experience of the sacrament of baptism? Other than having been baptized yourself, how have you participated in the sacrament?

2. How would you define baptism? What does the sacrament mean to you in terms of your Christian life?

3. Have you ever experienced infant baptism during Mass? What is your prayer for the infant as the child is carried through the assembly?

4. In thinking about your local parish, how would you characterize its pursuit for the unity of the Body of Christ in worship and in service to the world?

5. Try to imagine and propose creative ways in which Christians could work to promote a sense of unity within the Body of Christ while also preserving the diversity of the Church.

CHAPTER 2

Baptismal Leadership

In the church not everyone walks along the same path,
yet all are called to holiness and have obtained an equal
privilege of faith through the justice of God (see 2 Peter 1:1).
Although by Christ's will some are appointed teachers,
dispensers of the mysteries and pastors for others, yet all
the faithful enjoy a true equality with regard to the dignity
and the activity which they share in the building up of the
body of Christ.[1]

—*Lumen gentium*, 32

At the end of the first chapter, a king was defined as someone who rules. And Christ's model for ruling was described as that of servant leadership. Christ came not to be served but to serve (see Mark 10:45, Matthew 20:28, John 13:1–17). For many centuries, especially since the Protestant Reformation in the sixteenth century, there have been diverse ways of leading and organizing Christian communities for worship and work. The Roman Catholic Church, relying heavily on the sacraments and the visible manifestation of unity (that is, apostolic succession), is organized hierarchically. *Lumen gentium* begins its third chapter, "The Church Is Hierarchical," stating:

In order to ensure that the people of God would have pastors
and would enjoy continual growth, Christ the Lord set up in

---

1. LG, 32.

his church a variety of offices whose aim is the good of the whole body. Ministers, invested with a sacred power, are at the service of their brothers and sisters, so that all who belong to the people of God and therefore enjoy true Christian dignity may attain to salvation through their free, combined and well-ordered efforts in pursuit of a common goal.[2]

The *Dogmatic Constitution on the Church* is clear that pastors are chosen for the purpose of ordering the various ministries of the Church according to the posture of servant leadership. Thus, while the role of the pastor is indispensable for the organization of the Christian community, the building up of the Body of Christ is a work that belongs to all the baptized, and this building up takes place through the discernment of the Spirit's blessings. When we discover and identify the ways in which the Spirit has moved within the Church, we grow in maturity as Christ's Body. This is how all the members of the Body exercise their role as sharers in the ministry of Christ, priest, prophet, and king. This is how baptismal leadership is executed. Consider St. Paul's explanation in his First Letter to the Corinthians:

> There are different kinds of spiritual gifts, but the same Spirit; there are different forms of service but the same Lord; there are different workings but the same God who produces all of them in everyone. To each individual the manifestation of the Spirit is given for some benefit. To one is given through the Spirit the expression of wisdom; to another the expression of knowledge according to the same Spirit; to another faith by the same Spirit; to another gifts of healing by the one Spirit; to another mighty deeds; to another prophecy; to another discernment of spirits; to another varieties of tongues; to another interpretation of

---

2. LG, 18.

tongues. But the one and the same Spirit produces all of these, distributing them to each person as he wishes.[3]

In Paul's description of the distribution of gifts, he makes certain that the Spirit is recognized as the giver. While human recipients are meant to work with their gifts and develop them, they are better thought of as *stewards* of particular gifts rather than as "sole possessors." For this reason, it is most helpful when the members of the Body of Christ work together to call forth gifts that they witness within the membership of the Church.

When we recognize that each member of the Body of Christ has the duty of exercising leadership, we discover the importance of *discernment*. For the Body to grow and flourish, the members must discern together what gifts to best employ, given particular situations and moments in history. Sometimes, however, communal discernment is difficult and it takes a willingness to see the Christian life as an ongoing journey or pilgrimage. The Second Vatican Council's *Pastoral Constitution on the Church in the Modern World* (*Gaudium et spes* [GS]) envisions the work of the Church to always be "the responsibility of reading the signs of the times and of interpreting them in the light of the Gospel."[4] This document begins with a pastoral approach to understanding the world:

> The joys and hopes, the grief and anguish of the people of our time, especially of those who are poor or afflicted, are the joys and hopes, the grief and anguish of the followers of Christ as well. Nothing that is genuinely human fails to find an echo in their hearts. For theirs is a community of people united in Christ and guided by the holy Spirit in their pilgrimage towards the Father's kingdom, bearers of a message of salvation for all humanity.[5]

---

3. 1 Corinthians 12:4–11.

4. GS, 4.

5. GS, 1.

Discernment demands that the Church journey with people from every walk of life, truly trying to understand life from their perspective. Luke's story of the disciples on the road to Emmaus (Luke 24:13–35) is a perfect example of two followers of Jesus who have closed themselves off to the world because of their present grief, the death of the master teacher. However, the presence of a stranger who accompanies them along the way and who "opened the scriptures" (32) to them reveals the presence of the risen Lord in their midst. The discernment that took place, transforming grief-stricken hearts to ones that burned with new life, depended on an objective individual helping them to see reality in a truthful way. In the Emmaus story, we see that the fruit of good discernment is the recognition of the risen Lord's presence in the midst of his Body. This, in fact, is what all sacramental celebration is about, beholding the risen Christ alive in our midst. Such discernment is the work of Christian charity, discovering Christ in our neighbor.

Assuming that all baptized Christians have gifts that are meant to be used for the building up of the Body of Christ, how might we embrace discernment as a method for the calling forth of these gifts and for their use within the Church? Ladislas Orsy describes this form of baptismal leadership as follows:

> Each community within the Church is an organized body; it is alive when there is a dynamic interplay among the members. It must have a center where one (or several) person(s) clothed with authority stand and to whom informational data flow steadily from all directions. The task of the center is to create one mind and one heart in the community, out of the multiplicity of ideas and desires, in harmony with the aspirations of the universal Church. Such organic unity among intelligent persons cannot arise if those in authority alone decide all issues and call for an unconditional and blind surrender

in others. The ones who preside must respond in a spirit of service to the right and just desires of all.[6]

Perhaps the greatest contribution that Orsy's project makes for our consideration of baptismal leadership is his overall understanding that Christian discipleship is a journey involving change and growth. Just as we might say that baptism is a daily event that calls upon disciples to make a choice to follow the Lord, Orsy is clear that communal discernment focuses simply on helping the community make the next best step forward in life. He writes:

A Christian community is God's pilgrim people. He leads them by twists and turns toward the Promised Land. Their pilgrimage may include events analogous to those recounted in the Bible: the flight from Egypt, the hurried wading through the Sea of Reeds, the confused and seemingly aimless wandering in the desert, the perilous conquest of their new home against fierce resistance, and finally, the daily work of sowing seeds, planting vineyards, threshing wheat, and treading grapes. Our modern pilgrimage, no less than the old, is a journey into the unknown among many uncertainties. It requires much patience! God has his own way and no one can force his hand. Communal discernment is not meant to lay the future bare. Christ made no such promise to his disciples. . . . Community discernment, then, is not a means to detect the future. It has a different purpose: it helps the community to become aware of the next step and gives them the strength to take it—be it through the desert, in the battle, or in carrying out the mandate of bringing the good news to all people.[7]

Daily, Christians around the world pray the Lord's Prayer, a prayer of Christian pilgrimage and of discipleship, a prayer that

---

6. Ladislas Orsy, *Discernment: Theology and Practice, Communal and Personal* (Collegeville, MN: Liturgical Press, 2020), 7.

7. Orsy, 35.

marks each day as a new beginning. Not only do we ask God to sustain us with "daily bread" and to "forgive us" for our wrong-doings, but we also acknowledge that God's will "be done." Our role as Christian disciples is not to know the will of God at all times but rather to cooperate with the unfolding of God's will in our daily lives. Leadership based on our common baptism and rooted in the prayerful discernment of God's will, especially in interpreting how best to utilize the spiritual gifts that are a part of the Body of Christ, sees the Christian life from the perspective of service in a daily, communal journey.

It must be recognized that all have a part to play in exercising baptismal leadership.

For parish renewal to take place in the twenty-first century, the power and authority of our baptism must be reclaimed, and it must be recognized that all have a part to play in exercising baptismal leadership. Baptismal leadership involves discerning the gifts provided by the Spirit to the Body of Christ through the unique contributions of each of the baptized. Sharing in the priestly ministry of Jesus Christ calls for a willingness to cherish and promote the diversity of members within the Body, to be able to value that all parts are equal yet they look different and do different things. All contribute to the Body of Christ when consciously serving our brothers and sisters over themselves. Thus, the next chapter will explore how a serious commitment to attend to our baptismal calling and the dignity it provides leads to a transformation of relationships within the community that spills over into the Church's relationship to the larger society and the wider world.

❖ Discussion Questions ❖

1. In what ways do you exercise baptismal leadership when serving others?

2. Would you characterize your parish as a community that embraces the diversity of its members? If yes, what do you believe makes this hospitable attitude possible? If not, how could this situation be reversed?

3. Given the image of the Church as a pilgrim people, how do you approach life so as to live it as part of a larger journey?

4. What do you think about your baptism as involving daily discernment? How do you think your parish could improve its work as a discerning community?

5. If baptismal leadership involves discernment, what do you discern to be a primary gift that the Holy Spirit has bestowed upon you? In what ways might you be able to share this gift with the Body of Christ?

CHAPTER 3

Baptismal Transformation of the Christian Community

All must consider it their sacred duty to count social obligations among their chief duties today and observe them as such.
For the more closely the world comes together, the more widely
do people's obligations transcend particular groups and extend
to the whole world. This will be realized only if individuals and
groups practice moral and social virtues and foster them in
social living. Then, under the necessary help of divine grace,
there will arise a generation of new women and men, the mold-
ers of a new humanity.

—*Gaudium et spes*, 30

The Fathers of the Second Vatican Council were very much
aware of the negative effects of individualism in cultures
around the world that were influenced by capitalism and other forms
of development brought about through modernization. Although
they understood and praised the work of developing nations, they
also understood that such development often came with the price
of isolating individuals. Thus, they believed that the Church, by its
communal nature, has the obligation to challenge the social order:
"This communitarian character is perfected and fulfilled in the work
of Jesus Christ. . . . His command to the apostles was to preach the
Gospel to all nations in order that the human race would become

the family of God, in which love would be the fullness of the law."[1] Thus, the Church must organize itself to make unity a gift to be shared universally.

In the previous chapter, we saw that our common baptism and the leadership that results from it demands a unity in diversity that takes seriously the gifts that each baptized Christian offers for the building up of the Body of Christ. In turn, this demand suggests that the best model for baptismal leadership is one that is rooted in the discernment of gifts. Such a model envisions the Christian life as a daily event that unfolds gradually, meaning that discernment responds more as a next step rather than as a plan that attempts to predict the future. This chapter will examine ways in which leadership rooted in baptism, thus all the baptized, can serve to transform the Christian community and its commitments in the world.

Discerning the gifts of the baptized requires listening. All members of the Body of Christ must attempt to listen to each other to know and understand how other members ought best to be helped to fit into the community. Remember that the Body of Christ is all about relationships. When one person is brought into the community through baptism, the entire Body changes; when one person departs from the community through death, the entire Body changes. Discerning what is good for the whole requires listening to every part of the Body.

Ponder for a moment how the Church listens when it welcomes a stranger to its worship or welcomes again a member of Christ's Body who has been absent for whatever reason. If we are truly intent on extending the welcome of Christ, with arms and hearts wide open, then we strive to listen attentively and respectfully to all who do not fit into the majority or mainstream of the community. Consider those who participate in worship infrequently, who arrive and depart silently, those who are basically strangers. The parish

---

1. GS, 32.

needs to extend hospitality and show an openness to get to know those who are unknown. They belong to the Body of Christ, and they matter. As Bryan Cones and Stephen Burns write: "In effect, even while the language of 'diversity' and 'inclusion' may sometimes be sprinkled around the churches, liturgical practices of exclusion still dominate, propelling much human difference to the shadows of the liturgical assembly rather than drawing those who bear such difference to the centre, where they arguably belong."[2] To discern the gifts of the Body of Christ through listening, Christian disciples seek out the marginalized and those who appear different from the majority.

With this kind of work at its forefront, the Church is certain to become humbler, more accepting, more hospitable, all of which contribute positively to her mission of evangelization. Richard Gaillardetz has recently proposed the need for the Church to empty herself of any sort of divine privilege, thereby revealing the servant nature of the Church. He writes:

> We begin each celebration of the Eucharist with a penitential rite in which we profess our sinfulness and need for forgiveness, prayer and support; we confess our unworthiness before coming to the eucharistic table. These liturgical acts of repentance are more than an aggregation of individual confessions; they are *ecclesial* performances. Out of this penitential spirit and practice should arise an ecclesial humility that finds solidarity in the company of sinners and sees our church afresh in both its indefectible holiness and its undeniable sinfulness. A truly repentant and human church is a church that renounces moral superiority and exclusivism and encourages a spirit of hospitality toward all.[3]

---

2. Bryan Cones and Stephen Burns, "Introduction: The Vivid Richness of God's Image," *Liturgy with a Difference* (London: SMC Press, 2019), xiv.

3. Richard R. Gaillardetz, "Ecclesial Belonging in This Time of Scandal," *Worship* 94 (July 2020): 204.

The baptized are to witness to such hospitality and openness, thus inspiring others to follow in step. All members of the Body of Christ are called upon to scrutinize their demeanor and attitudes and to ask how they might provide a more accepting welcome of people from every walk of life. Such an examination is a matter of humble service.

Another issue that calls for a listening posture on the part of all members of the Body of Christ is the role of women in our Church. In the twenty-first century, with the prevalence of movements designed to challenge institutional structures that favor men over women, the Church needs to be vigilant and responsive regarding the conversation surrounding the voice and contribution of women in the Christian community. Given that women do not have equal positions of leadership in the hierarchy of the Catholic Church, it is much harder to hear, value, and represent their lived perspective. Although Pope Francis has reiterated the position that women cannot be ordained, he has made small steps in expanding the leadership role of women in the Church.[4]

If we believe that baptism into Christ establishes unity in diversity, the local parish needs to be a place where the voice of women is heard and given a role in discernment. For far too long, Scripture and tradition at times have been interpreted in such a way as to suggest that the suppression of women's voices is divinely willed and necessary for the natural order of things. Moreover, placing women on the margins has allowed for the development of the belief that men "are holier and more fully symbolic of Christ and God than women are."[5] Arguing that, more than ever before, the world needs the Church to be a sign and instrument of God's

---

4. See Elisabetta Provoledo, "Pope Formalizes Women's Roles, but Priesthood Stays Out of Reach," *The New York Times*, January 11, 2021. https://www.nytimes.com/2021/01/11/world/europe/pope-women.html.

5. Mary Doak, *A Prophetic Public Church: Witness to Hope amid the Global Crises of the Twenty-First Century* (Collegeville, MN: Liturgical Press, 2020), 91.

desire for the unity of all creation, with the exclusion of women being a countersign to this unity, theologian Mary Doak writes:

> The ongoing challenge for the church is to affirm the full equality of women and men on the one hand, while also making room for genuine difference, including differences that do not fit into a gender binary, on the other hand. . . . The point is not to deny sexual and gender differences but to embrace the full variety of healthy sexual embodiment as experienced across race, class, culture, ethnicity, and time. . . . A true ecclesial witness to unity-in-diversity is one that affirms gender plurality as a dimension of human embodiment in a way that reinforces rather than eclipses the fundamental Christian commitment to a common human nature and the equality of baptism.[6]

Subscribing to Paul's teaching that baptism strips away identity as male and female does not mean that women and men must approach life in the same way; rather, it means simply that their primary identity and their overarching worldview comes from their being molded into Christ. What is called for is an honoring of the unity in diversity that continues after baptism. If we honor one another as fellow members of Christ, then our differences are equally valued. Ensuring that women have an active voice in the work of discernment is fundamental if we are truly going to listen to the Body of Christ.

As the number of Catholics participating in regular Sunday liturgy continues to decline, with one recent poll estimating that only four out of ten Catholics attend Mass each week[7] (a statistic that has surely worsened as a result of COVID-19), it is all the more important that hospitality and welcome be extended in a renewed approach to ecumenism. Perhaps the downward trend in interest in

---

6. Doak, 111.

7. Gallup, "Catholics' Church Attendance Resumes Downward Slide," (April 9, 2018). https://news.gallup.com/poll/232226/church-attendance-among-catholics-resumes -downward-slide.aspx.

Sunday Mass (although not an excuse to remove it from the obligations of baptized Catholics) provides an opportunity to promote Christian engagement with the wider world with an ecumenical focus. The Fathers of the Second Vatican Council, having pronounced that "the restoration of unity among all Christians is one of the principal concerns"[8] of the Council, described the spirit of ecumenism as follows:

> Before the whole world let all Christians confess their faith in God, one and three, in the incarnate Son of God, our Redeemer and Lord. United in their efforts, and with mutual respect, let them bear witness to our common hope which does not play us false. Since cooperation in social matters is so widespread today, all people without exception are called to work together; with much greater reason is this true of all who believe in God, but most of all, it is especially true of all Christians, since they bear the seal of Christ's name. Cooperation among Christians vividly expresses that bond which already unites them, and it sets in clearer relief the features of Christ the Servant.[9]

Many Catholics struggle to believe in the description of the Christian community found in Ephesians: "[There is] one body and one Spirit, as you were also called to the one hope of your call; one Lord, one faith, one baptism" (4:4–5). Unfortunately, many believe that being baptized a Catholic is somehow "more Christian" than being baptized a Methodist or a Lutheran. Fortunately, such thinking is disappearing on a practical level as Catholics and other Christians cooperate side by side in so many life activities outside of religion. It is particularly important that Christians of different denominations learn from one another and that respect for our common baptism continues to grow.

---

8. *Unitatis redintegratio* (UR), 1.
9. UR, 12.

In so many ways, these points on baptismal transformation of our communities can be summed up in the understanding that baptism into Christ involves participation in the paschal mystery. The paschal mystery within liturgy is discussed frequently, but what does it mean to live the paschal mystery in our daily lives? It is so easy to profess with our lips that this is the central mystery of our faith, but do we truly understand what it demands of each of us? The paschal mystery is defined as the suffering, death, and resurrection of Christ, while our baptism means that we must share in this mystery. Our Christian lives are to embody a sacrificial nature. This is what it means to share in the priestly ministry of Christ. Just as Christ let go of life to live for others, so Christians must cease clinging to life as they know it for God to create them anew for others. Baptism is about shifting the focus away from ourselves to others; it is about seeing God's love as a gift not for me alone, but as tangibly alive for others as God builds up the unity of a diverse world. Mary A. Ehle beautifully writes:

> In a divided world, God's embrace of love at Baptism charges us with the responsibility to help bring about unity in the world while still respecting the marvelous, creative differences in everyone whom God has created. Asking ourselves how we can offer God's embrace of love to people in a world where many find themselves polarized from others politically, economically, socially, culturally, ethnically, and religiously is a question we must ask. The words and deeds of a Christian must serve to build unity in a diverse world that at its best is a reflection of the amazing love the three Divine Persons in the unity of God offers to us.[10]

---

10. Mary A. Ehle, *Anointed for Discipleship: The Meaning of Baptism for Our Christian Life* (Chicago: Liturgy Training Publications, 2019), 9.

It has been said that one of the most dangerous heresies ever to invade Christianity was that faith is a private affair and that it can be practiced completely on one's own. The truth is that Christianity is far from being a religion that can be lived out privately, neatly, and without the messiness of relationships. Just consider the mystery of the incarnation; God chose to experience firsthand the messiness of life! So too with the paschal mystery; Christianity involves embracing the reality of suffering and death for the sake of others. In our culture, we tend to disguise death and to avoid pain. Rather than taking on the lot of suffering, we want a quick fix. Our baptism asks us to approach life from the worldview of the Suffering Servant, who refuses to shirk the suffering imposed on him by the world, allowing the Father to transform that suffering into glory. Being a member of the Body of Christ demands that we honor all relationships united under the Head and that we embrace that the journey of life means that there will necessarily be messiness as relationships grow and change.

Contemplate the image of the Good Shepherd from the tenth chapter of the Gospel of John. Jesus proclaims himself to be the Good Shepherd, who "lays down his life for the sheep" (verse 11), who knows his sheep and his sheep know him (14), who has sheep from other flocks (16), and whose voice will be heard and followed by all because "there will be one flock, one shepherd" (16). A bond of unity exists between the Good Shepherd and the sheep because he roots his life in theirs, knowing their struggles, experiencing their pain. Our baptism demands a willingness to become immersed in the lives of others, to know their struggles, and to experience their pain. Pope Francis contends that

Our baptism demands a willingness to become immersed in the lives of others, to know their struggles, and to experience their pain.

an "evangelizing community" is composed of baptized leaders who "smell like the sheep." He writes in *The Joy of the Gospel (Evangelii gaudium* [EG]):

> An evangelizing community gets involved by word and deed in people's daily lives; it bridges distances, it is willing to abase itself if necessary, and it embraces human life, touching the suffering flesh of Christ in others. Evangelizers thus take on the "smell of the sheep" and the sheep are willing to hear their voice. An evangelizing community is also supportive, standing by people at every step of the way, no matter how difficult or lengthy this may prove to be. It is familiar with patient expectation and apostolic endurance. Evangelization consists mostly of patience and disregard for constraints of time. [11]

When Francis speaks about "evangelizers," he is not referring to the ordained alone, but to all who are called to preach the Gospel by virtue of their baptism. All the baptized share in the prophetic ministry of Christ and are thus called to "smell like the sheep." Baptism does not separate us from the world but immerses us ever deeper into its beating heart, as we bestow God's gifts of mercy and compassion upon the world. Discipleship requires an active and prayerful listening to the Good Shepherd, the Head of the Body. Everything that he embodies about a servant attitude is what we are to practice, sharing in his sacrificial spirit.

It is most fitting to call the Christian community "a pilgrim people." A pilgrim is someone who abandons self-focus and embraces a willingness to live in the moment. A pilgrim is one who lives in a sort of in-between space—neither here nor there—always seeking to move into the horizon. As Kevin Codd writes, "Life's difficult passages, sorrows, crosses, even deaths necessarily lead to new life in all kinds of surprising and glorious ways. Keeping an eye peeled for grace ahead guards us from despair. . . . We fall, we fail,

---

11. EG, 24.

we harm one another. Then we rise, we reconcile, we heal, and we continue down the road."[12] The pilgrim way embraces life as an ongoing process. Even when the pilgrim reaches the so-called destination, his or her pilgrimage is not over; it has just begun. So it is with our baptismal life. Each day is a choice to live as a disciple of Christ—to pick up, to heal, and to start anew.

As previously discussed, communal discernment of gifts is not meant to be far-reaching, it is meant to discover God's will for us at this very moment. The better we are at discerning and calling forth the gifts of all the members of the Body of Christ, the greater will be our ability to recognize the healing power of God's grace at every step of our pilgrim journey. Words from *Lumen gentium* close our reflection on baptism as the impetus for transforming our communities:

> All the members must be formed in his likeness, until Christ is formed in them (see Galatians 4:19). . . . On earth, still as pilgrims in a strange land, following in trial and in oppression the paths he trod, we are associated with his sufferings as the body with its head, suffering with him, that with him we may be glorified (see Romans 8:17).

> From him "the whole body, supplied and built up by joints and ligaments, attains a growth that is of God" (Colossians 2:19). He constantly makes available in his body, which is the church, gifts of ministries through which, by his power, we provide each other with the helps needed for salvation so that, doing the truth in love, we may in all things grow into him who is our head (see Ephesians 4:11–16, Greek).[13]

It is the Head of the Body, the Good Shepherd, who leads us on our pilgrim way, a journey that begins in our baptism and continues to

---

12. Kevin A. Codd, "'I Am a Pilgrim on the Earth': The Pilgrim Way," *Worship* 84 (2010): 169.

13. LG, 7.

unfold in our baptismal outlook each day of our lives until all creation is knit together as one in life eternal.

❖ Discussion Questions ❖

1. Believing that all of the baptized are bestowed with gifts by the Holy Spirit to be used for the building up of the Body of Christ, what are some of the gifts that you discern that you have been granted?

2. Do you see gifts in other members of the Body of Christ that do not seem to be put to good use? How might you engage in communal discernment to call forth these gifts and talents?

3. Pope Francis challenges those charged with responsibility to preach the Gospel (all baptized Christians) to "smell like the sheep." How do you actively engage in trying to understand the life situation of others in the community?

4. What concretely do you do to help the Church grow in unity and manifest this oneness in Christ to the world?

5. How do you think that your parish might best work to welcome those who feel alienated from the community?

PART 2

LIVING OUT OUR BAPTISMAL CALL

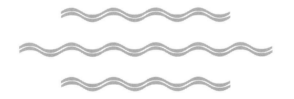

CHAPTER 4

The Door to Life and to the Kingdom

Amen, amen, I say to you, no one can enter the kingdom of God without being born of water and Spirit. What is born of flesh is flesh and what is born of spirit is spirit.
—John 3:5–6

In the context of the rich imagery Jesus employs in identifying himself as the Good Shepherd in the tenth chapter of John's Gospel is the statement: "I am the gate for the sheep" (10:7). While Jesus contends that the sheep know him, listen to his voice, and follow him (10:27), he also proposes that he is the "gate" through which his followers must pass to find pasture. A gate?

A gate, or a door, provides several functions. First, the threshold of a door is a place of choice. When a person stands in a doorway, he or she is neither in the interior or in the exterior space; instead, the person is in between. The technical term for this dimension of time and space is "liminality," a place or a time of transition. Thus, a gate is a place of discernment. One has to weigh carefully the consequences of entering versus remaining outside. Second, the door, as a passageway, provides a means of identification. One who has passed through the gate into the space that lies beyond may be considered to belong to that new location. Anthropologist Arnold van Gennep writes: "[T]o cross the threshold is to unite oneself with a new world."[1] Finally, a door provides a means of safety and protection for those inside. If the door is locked and well-fortified, it prevents outsiders from gaining entrance and prevents the insiders from wandering away. Jesus states: "I am the gate. Whoever enters through me will be saved, and will come in and go out and find pasture" (John 10:9).

Baptism involves (1) discerning a new way of life, (2) making the decision to cross over to a new world, and (3) discovering the security of freedom in Christ. Baptism introduces a Christian to the way of the paschal mystery and thus invites followers to put on a paschal approach to life. This new way of life means looking at death to self as the way to resurrected life. Without baptism, we have no means of participating in this new way of life. Canon 849 of the *Code of Canon Law* defines baptism as follows:

> Baptism, the gate to the sacraments, necessary for salvation in fact or at least in intention, by which men and women are freed from their sins, are reborn as children of God and, configured to Christ by an indelible character, are incorporated in the Church, is validly conferred only by washing with true water together with the required form of words.[2]

While there is a fair amount of legal speak in this definition of baptism, such as the requirements of "true water" and the "form of words," the theology within it is rich. Baptism provides an "indelible character" that cannot be stripped away as well as real incorporation into the Church that continues into the heavenly realm. Baptism provides identity and entrance. Once a person has been grafted onto Christ in baptism, hers is a new world that cannot be abandoned.

Ponder for a moment the placement of the baptismal font in many churches. It is well known that ancient baptisteries constructed

1. Arnold van Gennep, *The Rites of Passage* (Chicago: University of Chicago Press, 1960), 20.
2. *Code of Canon Law*, 849. (Washington, DC: Canon Law Society of America, 1983).

for the immersion of adult men and women were usually built as separate rooms very near the entrance of the worship space. The symbolic meaning of this placement is clear: one must pass through the sacrament of baptism to participate in the new life that lies within the community of Jesus' followers. Even when baptismal fonts are located in areas within the church building other than at the door, the waters of baptism continue to symbolize immersion into the new and exciting life that is adventure with Christ, or the life that we know as discipleship.

Not only does the baptismal font play a significant role in welcoming new members into Christ as well as reminding the baptized of their Christian duties, but the door itself plays an important role in marking life in Christ. Think about all the liturgical rites that the door silently witnesses. The *Order of Celebrating Matrimony* suggests that the liturgy begin with the priest greeting the couple at the door and that they process together to the altar. At the outset of the funeral liturgy, the priest welcomes the body of the deceased at the door of the church, and there sprinkles the casket with water and covers it with the pall, all done in remembrance of the moment the now-deceased Christian first entered the church through the sacrament of baptism. Thus, it is ideal that we witness infant baptisms beginning at the church door with the minister greeting the family and asking them for the name of the child to be baptized. Similarly, the *Rite of Christian Initiation of Adults* (RCIA) envisions the Rite of Acceptance opening as "the candidates, their sponsors, and a group of the faithful gather outside the church" to clearly designate this ritual as the moment of entrance into the journey of Christian faith.[3]

If a door clearly marks a place of discernment and new identity, then what about the security aspect? Doors and gates are designed to protect. They keep out what is not welcomed and keep in what wants to remain. Therefore, gates can be either hospitable

3. RCIA, 48.

or unwelcoming. If Christ is "the gate," then every door of the church—those of our church buildings and those of our hearts—must be hospitable.

In 2012, the Catholic bishops of the United States released a wonderful document entitled *Disciples Called to Witness: The New Evangelization*, in which they invite each parish to reimagine everything it is and does as being about the work of evangelization. At the forefront of evangelization is the need to provide a hospitable welcome, for as *Disciples Called to Witness* states: "The entire parish community, especially the parish leadership, must foster a spirit of hospitality and welcome."[4] Furthermore, the document suggests that opening the door in welcome takes place simply in the visible living of a corporate, Christian lifestyle:

> To create a culture of witness, we must live explicit lives of discipleship. Being a disciple is a challenge. Fortunately, one does not become a disciple on his or her own initiative. The work of the Holy Spirit within the Christian community forms the person as a disciple of Christ. . . .
>
> The commitment to living the Christian life provides an essential element of the culture of witness. To those seeking answers to the increasing secularization, individualism, and materialism of society, a Christian life provides a powerful witness to the Gospel. The public profession of one's faith through active participation in prayer, the sacraments, and especially Sunday Mass contributes to the sanctification of the world Additionally, the works of charity and justice as well as the promotion of solidarity, justice, peace, and stewardship of creation build up the Kingdom of God.[5]

---

4. *Disciples Called to Witness: The New Evangelization* (Washington, DC: United States Conference of Catholic Bishops, 2012), 17.

5. *Disciples Called to Witness*, 11–12.

Thus, a parish community that recognizes baptism as the door to life will focus on the attitude of hospitality in everything that it does. Simple acts of compassion done in the name of Christ have the possibility of igniting real transformation in the hearts of those we encounter. A parish must be built around the expectation that every member is called to be a hospitable (door-opening) representative of Christ and that all members see themselves as credible witnesses to the work of evangelization. All the baptized need to know that this is their Christian duty. As the introduction to

> A parish must be built around the expectation that every member is called to be a hospitable (door-opening) representative of Christ.

the *Rite of Christian Initiation of Adults* states ever so clearly: "[T]he people of God, as represented by the local Church, should understand and show by their concern that the initiation of adults is the responsibility of all the baptized. Therefore the community must always be fully prepared in the pursuit of its apostolic vocation to give help to those who are searching for Christ."[6] In reality, so much of providing a welcome in our parishes is about revealing the servant attitude of Christ, seeking to give up ourselves in the service of God's kingdom, demonstrating that the "royal priesthood" is a self-giving people. All who are baptized into Christ participate in keeping watch over the gate. We hope that those we invite through it will experience therein the true freedom Christ promises.

❖ Discussion Questions ❖

1. Describe the location of the baptismal font in your parish church. What does its shape and decoration communicate regarding entrance into Christ?

---

6. RCIA, 9.

2. What is your experience of hospitality at your local parish?

3. Baptism bestows identity and therefore belonging in Christ. What might your parish community do to promote a sense of belonging for those who might feel that they do not belong?

4. Active participation in the Sunday liturgy and the celebration of the sacraments is a form of evangelization. How do you see your participation as a means of witnessing to Christ's presence in the world?

5. What is your experience of the role of the community in the celebration of baptism? How might the members of the Body of Christ be more involved in the work of initiating new members into the Church?

CHAPTER 5

Built Up Together into a
Dwelling Place of God

As a body is one though it has many parts, and all the parts
of the body, though many, are one body, so also Christ.
For in one Spirit we were all baptized into one body, whether
Jews or Greeks, slaves or free persons, and we were all given
to drink of one Spirit.

—1 Corinthians 12:12–13

As stated at the outset of this work, the sacrament of baptism
has been celebrated as a private affair for far too much of
Christianity's existence. Because baptism became largely a sacrament for children to be washed from original sin, it lost most of
its connection to discipleship. Fortunately, the liturgical renewal
ushered in by the Second Vatican Council called for the retrieval of
the corporate dimension of the sacrament. This means that baptism
is not celebrated simply for the individual soul but for the Church as
a whole. Baptism is about entrance into the Church and communal
participation with all the members of the Body of Christ. The general introduction to *Christian Initiation* states quite clearly that
"Baptism is the Sacrament by which human beings are incorporated
into the Church and are built up together into a dwelling place of
God in the Spirit."[1]

---

1. *Christian Initiation*, general introduction, 4.

Recapturing the communal nature of the sacrament helps underscore a renewed understanding of grace. God's grace is not something that can be stockpiled and saved up to demonstrate personal righteousness. Nevertheless, many people think of grace like a bank account—the more grace they receive in the celebration of Mass or in the performance of works of charity, the more bonus points they compile to be cashed in for a place in heaven. This is not how divine grace works. Grace is union with God that is discovered by our life in Christ and rediscovered—not accumulated—on a daily basis. When baptism is celebrated in the context of a true Christian assembly (and not simply several family representatives), it becomes quite clear that grace involves active participation. God's grace abounds; we are meant to be attentive to it. God is willing to work with us, but we must be willing to do our fair share as well . . . together!

The obligation to participate in regular liturgical celebration is not for the purpose of individual Christians to prove themselves to be faithful to God as much as it is for Christians to come together to learn how to function as one, holy people, thus sharing in Christ's threefold office of priest, prophet, and king. Probing the depths of such union does not come easily to us in our world today as so much emphasis is put on the freedom to express one's uniqueness. It is more fashionable to stand out rather than to fit in. While always maintaining the importance of diversity, as Christians believe in a Triune God of diverse persons held together in perfect unity, we also must underscore and make visibly present our togetherness in Christ.

It is generally recognized that all liturgical prayer has at its core the celebration of the paschal mystery, defined as the suffering, death, and resurrection of Christ. However, it is seldom understood that remembering the paschal mystery (such as proclaiming the "mystery of faith" after the words of consecration in the Eucharistic Prayer at Mass) means that individual worshipers must work to surrender themselves by being reincorporated deeper and deeper into the worshiping assembly. When faith is professed in the risen Lord, who suffered, died, rose again, and promised to return to us, we are praying not as a collection of gathered individuals but as a *body* that attempts to recognize unity in Christ. All liturgy is designed to help us see more and more how our baptism demands a letting go of self to live anew for others. Liturgy strips us of our self-preoccupation and makes us one in Christ's Body.

Another way of talking about the corporate dimension of praying together as the Church, is that our communal prayer helps us discern the particular charisms that each member of the Body of Christ offers for the building up of the entire Church. That prayer, in turn, embraces the "joys and hopes, the grief and anguish"[2] of all the world's peoples as its own. Liturgical theologian Mark Searle likens this to being attentive to the working of God's justice. He writes:

> For the members of the worshipping community, relationships with one's fellow human beings are based not simply upon their common humanity but upon the common humanity as assumed and redeemed by the love and obedience of Jesus, and raised to a new level by the Spirit of Jesus at work in the world. . . . The liturgical assembly, at least in its ideal form, offers a model of such interaction. It is not a community of equals but a community of God-given and complementary charisms, gifts that cannot be identified *a priori* by categories of the secular community—age, sex, race—but are distributed indiscriminately among all for the sole purpose of building up the community in perfect justice.[3]

When the Spirit gathers the liturgical assembly to be re-membered in Christ (or to be put back together again in the risen Lord), the common worship is meant to rehearse the worldview of baptism,

---

2. GS, 1.

3. Mark Searle, "Serving the Lord with Justice," in *Liturgy and Social Justice*, ed. Mark Searle (Collegeville, MN: Liturgical Press, 1980), 24.

so that we learn to see the world as Christ sees it. In Searle's words, the liturgy "presupposes a group of people who can reach across the social, political, and economic barriers that structure our world to say, 'Our Father,' and to speak of themselves as a 'we.'"[4]

The demonstration of our oneness is precisely the reason the Second Vatican Council called for the restoration of various liturgical ministries within the Mass and other liturgical celebrations. The *Constitution on the Sacred Liturgy*, 28, states: "In liturgical celebrations, each one, minister or layperson, should do all of, but only, those parts which pertain to that office by the nature of the rite and the principles of liturgy." The performance of a liturgical ministry visibly manifests the belief that the Spirit provides members of Christ's Body with charisms that are used to build up the Church. If I am serving the Body of Christ as an usher, then I should not attempt to perform the ministry of a lector. If I am serving the Body of Christ as a member of the choir, then I should not fill in for an extraordinary minister of the Eucharist. If I am presiding at the altar, I should not usurp any of the liturgical ministries that are designed to build up the Body of Christ. The point is simple: we serve as ministers only because we have been gifted by the Spirit with a charism that is to be shared.

But what about those who discern that they are not called to public ministry in the Church? Is there a liturgical role that still pertains to them when they come to Mass on Sunday? Absolutely! Because the assembly may be considered to be a sacrament of Christ's presence, each member has a role to play in manifesting the unity that is his Body. As the *Constitution on the Sacred Liturgy* states:

> The Church earnestly desires that all the faithful be led to that full, conscious, and active participation in liturgical celebrations called for by the very nature of the liturgy. Such participation by the Christian people as "a chosen race, a royal

---

4. Searle, "Serving the Lord with Justice," 25.

priesthood, a holy nation, God's own people" (1 Peter 2:9; see 2–5) is their right and duty by reason of their baptism.[5]

Participation in Sunday Mass is required precisely because all baptized Catholics have the responsibility to build up the Body of Christ together. In other words, it makes a difference when members are absent. For this reason, the Church has always valued bringing Communion to the sick and the homebound; their presence within the assembly is sorely missed. However, for those called to be members of a liturgical assembly on any day, or at any time, calls for active participation. It demands that we spend some time preparing for the celebration, that we actively give ourselves over to all of the prayers, gestures, and moments of silence that the liturgy calls for, and that we dedicate time to reflect on our experience of the celebration after it concludes. Being a member of the assembly is a ministry of its own, it calls for self-sacrifice and work, and we must do everything we can to prevent ourselves from becoming merely spectators.

The same is true for ministries performed outside the context of the sacraments. Some people within the Body of Christ have been gifted with the charism of artistic talents. These are painters, craftsmen, potters, gardeners, landscapers, bakers, chefs, to name just a few. How are we to talk about these trades in terms of ministry? Take, for example, the spiritual gifts bestowed upon a landscaper. He or she can survey the beauty of the land and is able to discern how to best cooperate with the land to bring about

Whether gathered as an assembly of the faithful under the roof of a church building or out in the world as disciples using our gifts and talents to bring life and joy to others, we seek to unite this world together in love.

a new creation for the benefit of others. The role of the Body of Christ is to affirm this gift in people's lives, to name it, and to celebrate it in the context of the entire community, recognizing how this labor of love contributes to the flourishing of the Church in the world. Liturgy and life are seamless for the Christian. Thus, whether gathered as an assembly of the faithful under the roof of a church building or out in the world as disciples using our gifts and talents to bring life and joy to others, we seek to unite this world together in love. This is what it means to live out our vocation as disciples who share in Christ's identity as priest, prophet, and king.

❂ Discussion Questions ❂

1. How do you experience liturgy as a means of Christian formation?

2. Review the various acclamations for the proclamation of the mystery of faith during the Eucharistic Prayer. How do these words challenge us to relate to one another in the Body of Christ, as we all live out the paschal mystery?

3. The liturgical assembly is made into the Body of Christ through the work of the Spirit. How does the work of each member of the baptized contribute to the flourishing of this union?

4. Since all baptized Christians are called to "full, conscious, and active" participation in the liturgy, how do you prepare for Mass? How do you celebrate and reflect upon it?

5. The Church views liturgy and life as meant to be seamless. How do you connect regular participation in the Mass to the mission of Christ and, thus, the works of justice within the world?

CHAPTER 6

Adopted Sons and Daughters

For those who are led by the Spirit are children of God.
For you did not receive a spirit of slavery to fall back into
fear, but you received a spirit of adoption, through which
we cry, "Abba, Father!"

—Romans 8:14–15

The primeval account of the world's foundation, as described in chapter 1 of the Book of Genesis, reveals that God calls all creation "good." Every living plant, every drop of rain, every creature under heaven comes from the loving design of God and is meant to radiate beauty and praise back to the Creator. At the same time, Christians believe that baptism provides the human creation with the *status* of a new relationship of being called adopted sons and daughters of God. The general introduction to *Christian Initiation* states: "For having been incorporated into Christ through Baptism, they are formed into the People of God, and, having received the remission of all their sins and been rescued from the power of darkness, they are brought to the status of adopted sons and daughters. Hence they are called, and indeed are, children of God."[1] The word *status*, in this description of baptism, denotes not privilege but responsibility. Made one with Christ, Christians are necessarily responsible for the mission he left behind: "Go, therefore, make disciples of all nations" (Matthew 28:19).

---

1. CI, 2.

The designation of Christians as adopted children of God is intrinsic to the work of social justice. Take, for example, the Catholic social teaching on the theme of solidarity. In its simplest form, solidarity is the work of recognizing that all are part of one global family. There are no divisions brought about by race, nationality, gender, age, wealth; instead, all members of the human family are meant to be able to participate fully. It is even possible to say that solidarity demands the inclusion of a healthy relationship with natural resources and every creature God has made. Pope Francis writes in *The Joy of the Gospel*:

> The word "solidarity" is a little worn and at times poorly understood, but it refers to something more than a few sporadic acts of generosity. It presumes the creation of a new mindset which thinks in terms of community and the priority of the life of all over the appropriation of goods by a few. [2]

The change in mindset to which Pope Francis refers is about recognizing interdependence. Thus, being named an adopted son or daughter of God in no way is meant to call the Christian away from the world; instead, it necessarily demands a commitment to give oneself to the promotion of the common good. Baptism is not an escape from the world, but a deeper immersion into the pursuit of caring for all aspects of creation.

Another way of talking about solidarity is to say that sacrifice must be an important part of the Christian vocation. As discussed previously, sacrifice is a foundational facet of the paschal mystery, as we believe that Jesus chose the way of self-sacrifice over the way of self-preservation as a gift bestowed upon the Father. Sacrifice is furthermore based upon the fundamental right of human dignity—namely, that any form of poverty or oppression ought to be an offense to the children of God. Just as the Acts of the Apostles

---

2. EG, 188.

portrays the early Church as one in which all members worked to alleviate the needs of the poor (see Acts 2:45), so are Christians today meant to sacrifice to end poverty and hunger. That sacrifice means not simply providing a stopgap through charitable giving but demonstrating in action and through the conversion of lifestyle that Christians cannot allow the most vulnerable in society to slip through the cracks. Baptism demands that we work for a oneness in creation that is rooted in divine love. "In a world marked by extreme discrepancies between the rich and the poor," writes Bernard Evans, "the practice of solidarity necessarily calls for sacrifice."[3]

Recognizing the bonds of baptism that unite all the adopted children of God as brothers and sisters in the Lord is also intimately connected to the Church's teaching on the dignity of work and the rights of workers. When God completed the work of creation, he designated a day for rest, which would provide the opportunity for all that exists to take the time to contemplate the grandeur of creation as well as the abundant love of the Creator. Work is thus meant to be a sign of personal creativity as well as the accomplishment of an act of love for others. Just as God creates to give life, so is all human labor meant to be generative in nature. Rather than viewing work as drudgery and oppressive to the human spirit, the Church views work as a gift from God bestowed upon creation, so that we might be collaborators in perfecting his cosmic creation. The Second Vatican Council's *Pastoral Constitution on the Church in the Modern World* states, "When they (humans) work, not only do they transform matter and society, they also

Recognizing that we are all adopted children of God should awaken our hearts to labor for those who struggle to survive with dignity in our wider community.

---

3. Bernard Evans, *Glorifying the Lord by Your Life: Catholic Social Teaching and the Liturgy* (Chicago, IL: Liturgy Training Publications, 2020), 60.

perfect themselves. They learn, develop their faculties, emerging from and transcending themselves. Rightly understood, this kind of growth is more precious that any kind of wealth."[4]

Unfortunately, many people do not experience their work as fulfilling and transformative. For many people, labor is just a means of earning a paycheck that will be used to support a family and pay the bills. Rather than being self-expressive and creative, work can be alienating and life-draining. In such situations, parish membership could come together to generate possibilities for work on behalf of the Christian community that would allow for a creative expenditure of energy. Ponder this possibility: What if a parish were to organize a job fair that featured job openings in the surrounding communities? Members of the parish who own businesses or work as professionals could volunteer their time and expertise to meet with individuals to improve their resumes or could engage in mock interviews. Recognizing that we are all adopted children of God should awaken our hearts to labor for those who struggle to survive with dignity in our wider community. Gathering as brother and sister to repair the roof of a neighborhood widow, organizing a food drive, or tutoring in an aftercare program are simple ways in which to experience the generative nature of work.

Furthermore, our common baptism in the Lord demands that we must advocate for men and women who are underemployed. This is something that the gathered assembly should be regularly praying for in its intercessory prayer on Sunday, but it also demands a commitment to enact change within our society. The Catholic bishops of the United States, in their 1986 pastoral letter on economic justice, define the importance of the quality of work as follows:

> All work has a threefold moral significance. First, it is a principal way that people exercise the distinctive human capacity for self-expression and self-realization. Second, it is the ordi-

---

4. GS, 35.

nary way for human beings to fulfill their material needs. Finally, work enables people to contribute to the well-being of the larger community. Work is not only for oneself. It is for one's family, for the nation, and indeed for the benefit of the entire human family.[5]

Access to quality work provides one with the opportunity for greater participation within society and therefore the greater likelihood to be incorporated in a web of relationships. The bishops go on to suggest that "freedom, initiative, and creativity," which are all constituents of meaningful labor, are necessary in building up a healthy community. "The task of creating a more just U.S. economy is the vocation of all and depends on strengthening the virtues of public service and responsible citizenship in personal life and on all levels of institutional life."[6]

The moral imperatives of solidarity (or a spirit of interdependence) with the human community as well as with all of creation and the dignity of workers and labor in general are two aspects of Catholic social teaching that are intrinsically connected to baptism. Because the waters of baptism incorporate people into one Body as God's adopted sons and daughters, no one ought to escape our personal care and concern. Christians have a responsibility to act with justice for those not only within their parish community or in the civic community in which they live, but also for those who live in foreign lands thousands of miles away. Baptismal responsibility calls Christians to open their eyes daily to the realities of suffering and injustice that exist on the planet. To enact the priestly, prophetic, and kingly ministry of Christ is not to sit back and avoid getting involved; instead, Christians must be proactive in making the world that God created and called "good" a place of right relationship.

---

5. United States Catholic Bishops, *Economic Justice for All: Pastoral Letter on Catholic Social Teaching and the U.S. Economy* (Washington, DC: National Conference of Catholic Bishops, 1986), 97.

6. *Economic Justice for All*, 100.

◦ Discussion Questions ◦

1. How would you describe your personal relationship to work? If it is not life-giving or creative, what do you believe might help make it more so?

2. In what ways do you strive to reach out to nurture and support the lives of others in the community and beyond as called for by Catholic social teaching on solidarity?

3. What are the ministries available at your parish that seek to promote human dignity and to lift up the poor and those struggling to survive?

4. What creative ways might you design to bring Christians together to advocate on behalf of the unemployed and the underemployed?

5. How might the universal Catholic Church be better united in promoting the dignity of human life and labor?

CHAPTER 7

A Royal Priesthood, a Holy Nation

You are a "chosen race, a royal priesthood, a holy nation, a
people of his own, so that you may announce the praises" of
him who called you out of darkness into his wonderful light.

—1 Peter 2:9

The nineteenth chapter of the Book of Exodus contains a beauti-
ful description of the Israelites, who have recently been set free
from slavery in Egypt. God calls Moses to prepare himself and the
people in general for the reception of the covenant, which will serve
to bind God and the nation together as one for all generations to
come. The encounter unfolds as follows:

Moses went up to the mountain of God. Then the LORD called
to him from the mountain, saying: This is what you will say to
the house of Jacob; tell the Israelites: You have seen how I
treated the Egyptians and how I bore you up on eagles' wings
and brought you to myself. Now, if you obey me completely
and keep my covenant, you will be my treasured possession
among all peoples, though all the earth is mine. You will be to
me a kingdom of priests, a holy nation. That is what you must
tell the Israelites. So, Moses went and summoned the elders of
the people. When he set before them all that the LORD had
ordered him to tell them, all the people answered together,

"Everything the Lᴏʀᴅ has said, we will do." Then Moses brought back to the Lᴏʀᴅ the response of the people. (Exodus 19:3–8)

Here in the Book of Exodus, priestly identity as well as consecrated status depends upon keeping the covenant. It is God who will make of his people a holy nation; it is the people's responsibility to hold fast to the covenant. When Israel leaves Mount Sinai and begins a forty-year journey throughout the wilderness en route to the Promised Land, Israel would have to offer burnt sacrifices to God to visibly manifest its fidelity. The selection of choice animals and firstfruits for sacrifice by the priests of the Tabernacle gave witness to the people's ongoing trust in God's providential care.

Thus, what is called the "levitical priesthood" was comprised of men who participated in a ritual dedication, whereby those born into the priestly line of Aaron's family were set apart to offer sacrifice on behalf of the people.[1] Priests were adorned in elaborate vestments, worn so that they could be identified for the role they played in the community, a role that demanded the strict maintenance of purity. Consequently, holiness came to mean the ability to avoid defilement. It was not so much that these chosen men had a deeper relationship with God as much as it was that they were committed to stand before God in a state of ritual purity.

Lumen gentium employs the image of a priestly people early in the document, describing the Church as a sacred assembly far before considering her an ecclesial hierarchy. *Lumen gentium* describes the "priesthood of the faithful" as follows:

Christ the Lord, high priest taken from the midst of humanity (see Hebrews 5:1–5), made the new people, "a kingdom of priests to his God and Father" (Apocalypse 1:6; see 5:9–10). The baptized, by regeneration and the anointing of the holy Spirit, are consecrated as a spiritual house and a holy priest-

---

1. See the chapter in Exodus on the consecration of priests, Exodus 29.

hood, that through all their Christian activities they may offer spiritual sacrifices and proclaim the marvels of him who has called them out of darkness into his wonderful light (see 1 Peter 2:4–10). Therefore, all the disciples of Christ, persevering in prayer and praising God (see Acts 2:42–27), should present themselves as a sacrifice, living, holy and pleasing to God (see Romans 12:1). They should everywhere on earth bear witness to Christ and give an answer to everyone who asks a reason for their hope of eternal life (see 1 Peter 3:15). [2]

Two important distinctions need to be made between the "priesthood of the faithful" and the ancient pattern and practice of priesthood of the old covenant. First, instead of sacrificing animals, disciples of Christ are called to offer their entire lives as a sacrifice to God. The priestly duty of offering up to God continues to apply to all the baptized; their offering is not cattle or sheep, but a humble and contrite heart. [3] Second, unlike the Levites of the Israelite community, who needed to maintain a distance from the ordinary lives of the members of the tribe to preserve their holiness, *Lumen gentium* declares that the priesthood of the faithful is to testify to Christ "everywhere on earth." The call to holiness is not an invitation to dwell apart from others but rather to radiate Christ's presence in every part of the world. Mary A. Ehle outlines the diverse ways in which Christians respond to the call to holiness by enacting their role as a priestly people:

> Daily we live as priestly people when we reflect on how we make present the holiness and sacredness that is inside of us

The call to holiness is not an invitation to dwell apart from others but rather to radiate Christ's presence in every part of the world.

2. LG, 10.

3. See Psalm 51.

and then act accordingly. When we honor the holiness and sacredness in every man, woman and child we encounter by speaking words that build others up rather than tear them down, we acknowledge the holiness within all God's people. When we lead prayer in our communities, in small groups, in our homes, and among our friends we embody our identity as members of God's priestly people. We do this when we offer ourselves and the gifts of bread and wine to become the Body and Blood of Christ at Mass. When we pray for the needs of others and for their salvation. And, when our prayer invites and welcomes the stranger, the immigrant, the homeless, and the brokenhearted to participate, we recognize how our holiness merges with theirs and together we can seek new ways of loving one another and affirming the holiness inside of us.[4]

Every member of the priesthood of the faithful, all baptized members of the Body of Christ, are called to pursue a life of holiness in the world. The Church needs the ordained to minister the sacraments and to provide leadership within the Body of Christ, but all the baptized must exercise a priestly ministry of service. While Pope Francis has reminded the ordained that their ministry "is not a career, but it is a service,"[5] equally necessary is for all the baptized to exercise their priestly service as well. Perhaps at this point in the history of the world, when people of so many diverse perspectives on life are linked in a globalized network of relationships, it is more necessary than ever to identify the servant nature of lay leadership in our Church. The Church needs to make a difference in a secular society that is quickly losing sight of the divine. Baptism demands that Christian disciples bring the light of Christ into the darkened world. *Lumen gentium* states:

---

4. Ehle, 14.

5. Pope Francis, "Pope Francis to New Priests: Be Servants, not Careerists" (https://www.americamagazine.org/faith/2021/04/26/prayer-be-poor-new-priests-pope-francis-240541). Last accessed June 7, 2021.

To be secular is the special characteristic of the laity. . . . It is the special vocation of the laity to seek the kingdom of God by engaging in temporal affairs and directing them according to God's will. They live in the world, in each and every one of the world's occupations and callings and in the ordinary circumstances of social and family life which, as it were, form the context of their existence. There they are called by God to contribute to the sanctification of the world from within, like leaven, in the spirit to the Gospel, by fulfilling their own particular duties. Thus, especially by the witness of their life, resplendent in faith, hope and charity they manifest Christ to others. It is their special task to illuminate and order all temporal matters in which they are closely involved in such a way that these are always carried out and develop in Christ's way and to the praise of the Creator and Redeemer.[6]

Lay men and women perform the prophetic function of Christ's ministry when they strive to proclaim the truth of the Gospel "in temporal affairs," thereby "directing them according to God's will." In other words, all the baptized are commissioned in their words and actions to bring the good news of Christ into the workplace, the school, the playground: in short, the entire world in which they are immersed. Similarly, the priesthood of the faithful is exercised when disciples strive to manifest the paschal mystery of Christ in their lives, when they choose the way of death to selfishness and ego in order to live unencumbered for others. Christians are to learn, on a daily basis, that the suffering of the cross promises to bring the resurrection of Easter. The way of holiness is discovered not only by weekly participation in the Eucharist but in the challenge to live as selflessly as Christ. Together, as a priestly people, we are called to shine forth in the world as a holy nation.

---

6. LG, 31.

✿ Discussion Questions ✿

1. How is your life a prayer of thanksgiving? How do you act as a priest when lifting up the needs and the concerns of the world to God?

2. Sharing in Christ's priestly ministry to heal, how do you participate in charitable deeds that involve personal sacrifice for others?

3. The family is often referred to as the *domestic church*. How is prayer a part of your household? Do you and your family read Scripture together, or do you gather to pray the Rosary or keep some other Christian devotion?

4. How do you and your parish actively engage in supporting the health and holiness of those called to serve the Body of Christ as ordained priests?

5. How does parish leadership promote the vocation of the lay faithful by summoning and nurturing their call to holiness?

CHAPTER 8

Responding to the Gospel of Christ

"But you will receive power when the Holy Spirit comes upon you, and you will be my witnesses in Jerusalem, throughout Judea and Samaria, and to the ends of the earth." When he had said this, as they were looking on, he was lifted up, and a cloud took him from their sight. While they were looking intently at the sky as he was going, suddenly two men dressed in white garments stood beside them. They said, "Men of Galilee, why are you standing there looking at the sky?"

—Acts of the Apostles 1:8–11

The proclamation of the good news of Jesus Christ is an urgent affair placed upon the shoulders of every baptized disciple. Once one has encountered the risen Lord in the hearing of his Word and has given oneself over to the project of following Christ (a commitment made tangibly present in the sacrament of baptism), preaching the Gospel to others is a must. The urgency with which the Gospel must be taken out into the world is demonstrated in the opening scene of the Acts of the Apostles. Immediately prior to his ascension, the Lord charges the apostles to be his witnesses "to the ends of the earth" (1:8). Instead of going right to work, they are caught gazing up at the sky. Two men questioned them as if to ask: "Well, what are you waiting for?"

This question must confront each baptized Christian daily: "What are you waiting for?" Pope John Paul II readily acknowledges the seriousness of carrying the Gospel out into the world in his 1991 *Redemptoris missio*:

> The mission *ad gentes* faces an enormous task, which in no way is disappearing. Indeed, both from the numerical standpoint of demographic increase and from the socio-cultural standpoint of the appearance of new relationships, contacts and changing situations the mission seems destined to have ever wider horizons. The task of proclaiming Jesus Christ to all peoples appears to be immense and out of all proportion to the Church's human resources.[1]

While relationships are more and more enacted on a global stage rather than localized in the context of a tight-knit community (for instance, the ability to connect virtually and so very easily with people in all corners of the globe), the requirement to make Jesus known, loved, and served is made all the more difficult in our fast-paced world. In the 1975 encyclical *Evangelii nuntiandi*, Pope Paul VI wrote of a "lack of fervor" in the work of Christian evangelization and the obstacles that stand in its way: "fatigue, disenchantment, compromise, lack of interest and above all lack of joy and hope."[2]

It is important to underscore, once again, that the task of evangelization belongs to every baptized Christian. One is baptized to share in Christ's ministry of prophecy. Too often the clergy are considered the experts in the field of evangelization, with many parishioners seeing themselves as inadequately prepared for preaching the Gospel. Even when the work of evangelization is explained as encompassing *how* one goes about mundane daily tasks or *how* one conducts oneself in the work setting, the vast majority of Christians continue to believe that evangelization is the work of missionaries

---

1. John Paul II, *Redemptoris missio*, 35.

2. Paul VI, *Evangelii nuntiandi*, 80.

or those who occupy the pulpit on Sundays. Even the way in which many parishes are organized betrays the universal mission to be evangelizers; just consider the way in which the *Rite of Christian Initiation of Adults* is deemed a parish-sponsored program rather than the very life of the parish itself. Catholics need to learn to think of our parishes as evangelizing communities, with everyone witnessing to the joy of the Gospel.

Perhaps one of the most vital areas where a sound revelation of the good news needs to take place is in married life and families. There is no denying that marriage is a fragile institution in our world. Divorce is sometimes chosen before any serious efforts are made to reconcile. Families are also fragile, as members of the household occupy themselves with commitments outside the home and make little effort to spend time together as a family. In both marriage and family life, the Gospel needs to be heard, discerned, and followed. The Catholic bishops of the United States have written: "The family, called the domestic Church, is often the first place where one experiences and is formed in the faith. . . . It is through the example of mothers and fathers, grandparents, siblings, and extended family members that one most concretely witnesses how to live a Christian life."[3] Exerting a commitment to work on family relationships is a form of preaching the Gospel.

It should be quite obvious that our common baptism unites us in the ministry of living the Gospel message with joy. It is not simply that I live joyfully, but that the entire Body of Christ radiates a love for the world that flows from a deep penetration of the Gospel message. In this way, each activity and organization, every minister both lay

Responding to the Gospel is what the leaders and participants of youth ministry programs do when they gather for an evening of fun at the bowling alley.

3. *Disciples Called to Witness*, 13.

and ordained, all work together to form a community that is hard at work evangelizing. Responding to the Gospel is what members of the altar and rosary society do when they provide fresh flowers to adorn the altar. Responding to the Gospel is what the leaders and participants of youth ministry programs do when they gather for an evening of fun at the bowling alley. Responding to the Gospel is what volunteers at a soup kitchen do when they serve meals to the homeless. In these and every work involving parish membership, what matters is that we witness to the love and joy of Christ. In the 2013 apostolic exhortation *The Joy of the Gospel*, Pope Francis describes what it means to be an "evangelizing community":

> The Church which "goes forth" is a community of missionary disciples who take the first step, who are involved and supportive, who bear fruit and rejoice. . . . Such a community has an endless desire to show mercy, the fruit of its own experience of the power of the Father's infinite mercy. . . . An evangelizing community is always concerned with fruit, because the Lord wants her to be fruitful. It cares for the grain and does not grow impatient at the weeds. The sower, when he sees weeds sprouting among the grain does not grumble or overact. He or she finds a way to let the word take flesh in a particular situation and bear fruits of new life, however imperfect or incomplete these may appear. The disciple is ready to put his or her whole life on the line, even to accepting martyrdom, in bearing witness to Jesus Christ, yet the goal is not to make enemies but to see God's word accepted and its capacity for liberation and renewal revealed. Finally an evangelizing community is filled with joy; it knows how to rejoice always. It celebrates every small victory, every step forward in the work of evangelization.[4]

---

4. EG, 24.

Interestingly enough, Pope Francis suggests that the work of evangelization on the part of all disciples is a matter of first getting involved.[5] The more Christians are involved in the life of the parish, the more likely they will see the difference they make in helping the world to see Christ. Instead of relying upon a small cohort of parishioners who seem to be actively involved in everything that the parish does, each person needs to step forward and participate. First, the gifts the Spirit has given are discerned, and then those gifts are put to good use in building up the Body of Christ.

A simple suggestion to help parishioners feel more connected to the work of evangelization is to encourage frequent reading of and reflection upon Scripture. To begin with, the readings for the coming Sunday should appear in every bulletin so that parishioners might be led to prepare for Mass by reading these biblical passages ahead of time. Furthermore, every parish could organize gatherings for Christians to come together to read and study the Bible, an activity that could be open to Christians of all denominations. Moreover, all parish meetings ought to involve some engagement with the Bible. Whether it be a monthly committee meeting of the liturgy or finance committee, or catechetical or social gatherings such as evenings with parents preparing for the baptism of their children, or a gathering of quilters sewing a quilt for a parish fundraiser, where two or three are gathered in Christ's name, the Word of God ought to be heard.

One of the formulas for the dismissal at the end of the Mass, new to the most recent edition of the missal, proclaims: "Go forth, glorifying the Lord by your LIFE."[6] This command is made to the gathered Body of Christ, which is now sent out into the world as one to proclaim the Word in all that we do. It is quite problematic that the Body breaks up and disperses as quickly as it does, as individual

5. EG, 24.

6. Capitalization is mine.

Christians hurry off to the golf course or the grocery store. However, even though quickly dispersed, the Body is still united as one by the Word that they have heard and have said *yes* to in their common Communion. There are so many ways that we repeat that "Amen" in our daily lives throughout the week, and there are even more opportunities that we might take to share that Word with others. Let us heed the plea of Pope Francis:

> Evangelization demands familiarity with God's word, which calls for dioceses, parishes and Catholic associations to provide for a serious, ongoing study of the Bible, while encouraging its prayerful individual and communal reading. We do not blindly seek God, or wait for him to speak to us first, for "God has already spoken, and there is nothing further that we need to know, which has not been revealed to us." Let us receive the sublime treasure of the revealed word.[7]

⚬ Discussion Questions ⚬

1. In what ways do you see your words and your actions as forms of preaching the good news of Jesus Christ?

2. How might you better incorporate the study of the Bible as part of your parish ministry? Of your daily life with the family? Of your own personal contemplation?

3. How might your parish organize itself to have a more prophetic voice in the local community through word and action?

---

7. EG, 175.

4. Would you label your parish an "evangelizing community"? If so, what specifically contributes to this preaching of the Word? If not, what might the parish do to summon each baptized disciple to a sense of responsibility for evangelization?

5. In celebrating the Mass, do you understand the way in which the faithful are sent into the world as one, united Body of Christ? What do you do personally to keep those bonds of union strong during the week?

CHAPTER 9

Built Up Together in the Spirit

> [You are] built upon the foundation of the apostles and
> prophets, with Christ Jesus himself as the capstone. Through
> him the whole structure is held together and grows into a
> temple sacred in the Lord; in him you also are being built
> together into a dwelling place of God in the Spirit.
>
> —Ephesians 2:20–22

In the early Church, as well as in the contemporary *Rite of Christian Initiation of Adults*, the sacramental washing in the waters of baptism is followed immediately by the anointing with chrism (confirmation) and then the gathering around the Lord's table to break the bread and share the cup (Eucharist). Hence the ancient pattern of initiation: baptism, confirmation, Eucharist, all celebrated in one ritual event. There is a structural unity to the sacraments of initiation when they are celebrated as part of one rite, with confirmation sealing baptism and Eucharist as the completion of Christian initiation. The *Catechism of the Catholic Church* states: "The holy Eucharist completes Christian initiation. Those who have been raised to the dignity of the royal priesthood by Baptism and configured more deeply to Christ by Confirmation participate with the whole community in the Lord's own sacrifice by means of the Eucharist."[1] Notice the role of the Spirit in this sacramental movement—it is the Spirit who seals Baptism and the Spirit who

---

1. *Catechism of the Catholic Church*, 1322.

leads one to the Eucharist. The Spirit's role is to draw us ever deeper into the life of Christ.

Many Catholic Christians are unaware of the ancient order of initiation just presented. The experience of most Catholics follows the order of celebrating baptism in early infancy, partaking in first Communion at the age of reason (or seven years old), and celebrating confirmation as the end of initiation in adolescence (or around the age of fifteen). Catholics tend to image the sacraments of initiation as stepping-stones to be received as one matures along the Christian way. However, what usually happens when the sacraments are spread out over the course of one's childhood is that we begin to conceive of them as achievement awards bestowed upon us to mark our progress. But the sacraments of initiation, indeed all the sacraments of the Church, are neither about us nor about what we have accomplished. They are about Christ and what he is accomplishing in us for the salvation of the world. For this reason, it is impossible for us to claim that we have completed our initiation. Christians are never finished maturing in their life with Christ; there is always more to learn, always more to be discovered.

When we see clearly confirmation in connection with baptism—namely, as the sacrament that seals and paves the way to the celebration of the Eucharist—not only will we understand the need to reunite and reorder these initiation sacraments, but we will also come to a better appreciation of the working of the Holy Spirit throughout our Christian lives. Then it will be realized that the Holy Spirit pours gifts upon us each day. Furthermore, through the work of discernment with other disciples, we will come to the realization that the gifts of the Spirit are not necessarily static, meaning that we stand to be given new gifts at every turn in the road. Let us consider for a moment the working of the Holy Spirit in the baptism of the Lord as recorded in Mark's Gospel:

It happened in those days that Jesus came from Nazareth of Galilee and was baptized in the Jordan by John. On coming up out of the water he saw the heavens being torn open and the Spirit, like a dove, descending upon him. And a voice came from the heavens: "You are my beloved Son; with you I am well pleased." At once the Spirit drove him out into the desert, and he remained in the desert for forty days, tempted by Satan. He was among wild beasts, and angels ministered to him. [2]

This passage, the earliest testimony to Jesus's baptism, suggests that the Spirit serves two basic functions in relationship to the Lord. First, the Spirit provides some visible sign that accompanies the Father's voice in announcing the presence of his Son. Just as in the story of Noah's sending the dove forth from the ark to testify to the dried earth (Genesis 8:6–12), so too is a dove associated with the regeneration of creation inaugurated at the Lord's baptism. In Jesus the covenant is restored, and the world begins anew. The second role of the Spirit in the account of Jesus' baptism is to send Jesus into mission, which begins with a time of formation in the desert. Thus, the Spirit participates both in making known the presence of the Lord and in the guidance of his mission.

Why should we expect it to be any different for us, we who follow the Lord as disciples? The Holy Spirit continues to operate in the Church in exactly the same way. The Spirit has the dual role of strengthening the unity of members in Christ and in guiding this Body, the Church, into mission. Think about the celebration of the Mass. The prayer that precedes the institution narrative, known as the *epiclesis*, calls for the Spirit's descent upon the gifts of bread

The working of the Spirit helps to remind us that all our labor in sowing together the world in mercy and love is the work of the Lord.

---

2. Mark 1:9–13.

and wine. This is done so that the Church may be able to see the presence of Christ in the gift that he left us. Thus, the praying assembly asks the Father to make the Lord present to the community in a tangible way. By faith, we believe the Spirit acts on our behalf.

However, the Spirit does not simply open our eyes to the presence of Christ in our midst; the Spirit unites us together in Christ so that we might be sent in mission. This is the Spirit's second function. The faithful consume the Body and Blood of the Lord to grow deeper into his identity and to be commissioned anew to be sent forth into the world as "one body, one Spirit in Christ."[3] These two functions of the Holy Spirit serve to unite our daily work of discipleship with our participation in Christ's identity that is established at baptism. Not simply doing good works, we are working together in Christ to build up the kingdom on earth. The working of the Spirit helps remind us that all our labor in sowing together the world in mercy and love is the work of the Lord. Our labor for the kingdom is inseparable from our common identity in Christ. Thus, the gifts of the Holy Spirit celebrated in the sacrament of confirmation are not bestowed upon us as personal property but rather as seeds for sowing the mission.

Let us consider the gifts of the Spirit that are mentioned as part of the order of confirmation. The prayer that accompanies the laying on of hands at the celebration of confirmation within the context of the Easter Vigil reads as follows:

> Almighty God, Father of our Lord Jesus Christ,
> who brought these your servants to new birth
> by water and the Holy Spirit,
> freeing them from sin:
> send upon them, O Lord, the Holy Spirit, the Paraclete;
> give them the spirit of wisdom and understanding,

---

3. See Eucharist Prayer III.

the spirit of counsel and fortitude,

the spirit of knowledge and piety;

fill them with the spirit of the fear of the Lord.

Through Christ our Lord.[4]

This prayer mentions both our identity and our mission as Christian disciples. First, our identity. We are set free from a relationship with sin to experience the new life of a relationship as God's sons and daughters. Alluding to our baptism ("water and the Holy Spirit"), this prayer suggests that discipleship entails the discernment of how the Holy Spirit acts in our lives to help and guide us. Thus, our mission. Wisdom, understanding, counsel, fortitude, knowledge, piety, and fear of the Lord are not poured upon us to puff us up, like weights in a gym that help muscles strengthen and grow. These gifts are about our relationship in Christ. They are all meant to be used in service.

Discerning the gifts of the Spirit is no easy task, which is precisely why it is best undertaken together. As discussed earlier in this work, communal discernment is what helps keep the Church on her pilgrim journey. As theologian Susan Wood writes: "We assume our place in the order of the Church according to our stage in life and the charisms we bring for the building up of the community and Christian discipleship."[5] The Spirit builds us up together in the Lord, and together we work to reveal the Lord's saving and healing presence in our world. "Discipleship is not an achievement," writes Kathleen Cahalan, "It is an identity, a commitment, a way of life, and a response to a call."[6] How do you respond to God's call?

---

4. RCIA, 234.

5. Susan K. Wood, "Conclusion: Convergence Points toward a Theology of Ordered Ministries," in *Ordering the Baptismal Priesthood: Theologies of Lay and Ordained Ministry*, ed. Susan K. Wood (Collegeville, MN: Liturgical Press, 2003), 257.

6. Kathleen A Cahalan, "Toward a Fundamental Theology of Ministry," *Worship* 80 (2006): 115.

❂ Discussion Questions ❂

1. How does your parish make tangible God's call to ministry and discipleship?

2. What gifts do you believe the Holy Spirit is pouring upon you so that you might offer them for the building up of the Body of Christ?

3. In what ways do you encourage others to respond to the action of the Spirit in their lives to minister as disciples in the Church?

4. What are some of the concerns or needs in your community that seem to go unaddressed by Christian service? How might the parish organize itself to better respond to these needs and concerns?

5. Attempt to tell the story of your lived experience as a Christian disciple. What are some of the joys and struggles that you have lived through in your following of Christ?

CHAPTER 10

Baptism as the Bond of Unity

Baptism, therefore, establishes a sacramental bond of unity among all who through it are reborn.

—*Decree on Ecumenism*, 22

When the bishops of the Roman Catholic Church gathered in the mid-1960s to examine how to renew the Church, one of the topics on their agenda was the issue of ecumenism, or how the Catholic Church relates to Christians of other denominations. At that time in history, it was quite common for Catholics to be heavily influenced by the expression "outside the Church, there is no salvation" (*extra ecclesiam nulla salus*). Associated with the writings of Cyprian of Carthage in the third century,[1] this term came to be applied not only to non-Christians but to Christians who were separated from the Catholic Church as a result of the Protestant Reformation in the sixteenth century.

Such exclusivism, while certainly diminished in our world today, continues to be problematic for Christian relations. While the Catholic Church promotes a sense of unity with other Christians, many continue to consider non-Catholics as second-class Christians, somehow lacking in the fullness of faith. In 1939, ecclesiologist (a theologian who studies the nature of the Church) Yves Congar wrote that true ecumenism means believing that a non-Catholic

---

1. See Ormond Rush, *The Vision of Vatican II: Its Fundamental Principles* (Collegeville, MN: Liturgical Press, 2019), 372.

Christian is a Christian not *in spite* of his or her separated community of faith but *because* of it. Congar contends:

> Ecumenism begins when it is admitted that others, not only individuals but ecclesiastical bodies as well, may also be right though they differ from us; that they too have truth, holiness and gifts of God even though they do not profess our form of Christianity. There is ecumenism, says an active member of this movement, when it is believed that others are Christians not in spite of their particular confession but in it and by it. Such a conviction governs that complex of ideas which make up the ecumenical attitude—respect for other confessions and the action of the Holy Spirit in them, the sense and the avowal of the past sins, limitation and failures of one's own confession, the desire to know about the other confessions and the gifts of God to them and to enter into friendly relations with them, and, pending full unity, as far as possible into effective communion.[2]

Congar's description of true ecumenism demands a shift in attitude that Catholics today still need to make. While it is true that the radical separation that constituted the relationships between Catholics and Protestants in the middle of the twentieth century has softened tremendously—witnessed simply in the ease of families condoning and celebrating interdenominational marriages today—does there not remain a lingering air of superiority on the part of many Catholics? In other words, is it not the case that ecumenism for many Catholics means luring other Christians into the Catholic fold?

It must be recognized that a truly ecumenical attitude comes down to believing that the Holy Spirit gifts other Christians just as much as Catholic Christians, "when it is believed that others are Christian not in spite of their particular confession but in it and

---

2. Yves Congar, *Divided Christendom: A Catholic Study of the Problem of Reunion* (London: Geoffrey Bless, 1939), 135–136. Quote taken from Rush, *The Vision of Vatican II: Its Fundamental Principles* (Collegeville, MN: Liturgical Press), 373–374.

by it." Congar suggests that an ecumenical attitude consists of the following:

* respect for the working of the Holy Spirit in other Christian communities;
* admission of the past sins and failures in one's own church;
* learning about other ways of approaching the Christian faith;
* establishing friendly relations based on dialogue and prayer.

Our common baptism calls us to promote an ecumenical spirit in all things, and that takes work and sacrifice. One cannot truly learn about other Christian communities and understand them if he or she approaches this study by holding on to the belief that Catholicism holds the only truth. Ecumenism requires genuine openness and humility. This is demanded by the very nature of our baptism into Christ as brother and sisters in the Lord.

The Second Vatican Council's *Decree on Ecumenism* is clear in the way in which effort should be taken to join hands with all Christians and learn from them our differences and our similarities. Furthermore, it suggests that there is much that diverse Christians can do together to carry out the work of building up the world in unity:

> The Christian way of life of these our sisters and brothers is nourished by faith in Christ. It is strengthened by the grace of baptism and by hearing the word of God. This way of life expresses itself in private prayer, in meditation on the scriptures, in the life of a Christian family, and in the worship of the community gathered together to praise God. Furthermore, their worship sometimes displays notable features of a liturgy once shared in common. The faith by which they believe in Christ bears fruit in praise and thanksgiving for the benefits received from the hands of God. Joined to it is a lively sense of justice and a true charity toward others. This active faith has

been responsible for many organizations for the relief of spiritual and material distress, the advancement of the education of youth, the improvement of social conditions of life, and the promotion of peace throughout the world.[3]

Notice that this paragraph never mentions the word *doctrine*. It suggests instead that commonality, or a sense of unity in diversity, may be discovered in discerning the Christian life (that is, the ways in which Christians might come together to educate, to heal, to pray, and to promote justice and peace throughout the world). As Pope Francis has written:

> The true defenders of doctrine are not those who uphold its letter, but its spirit; not ideas but people; not formulae but the gratuitousness of God's love and forgiveness. . . . The Church's first duty is not to hand down condemnations or anathemas, but to proclaim God's mercy, to call to conversion, and to lead all men and women to salvation in the Lord.[4]

Following Congar's agenda of respect, contrition, education, and friendship through dialogue and prayer, Christians can do so much together to show the desire to develop the unity marked by our shared baptism. Ponder this question for a moment: When was the last time you heard a homily that addressed the need to work on respect and friendship with Christians outside the Catholic

Christians need to come together in prayer and to celebrate what makes us different as well as to celebrate what makes us one.

---

3. UR, 23.

4. Pope Francis, "Address at the Conclusion of the Synod of Bishops" (October 24, 2015). http://www.vatican.va/content/francesco/en/speeches/2015/october/documents/papa-francesco_20151024_sinodo-conclusione-lavori.html. Quote found in Richard R. Gaillardetz, "Ecclesial Belonging in This Time of Scandal," *Worship* 94 (July 2020): 201–202.

Church? Are we taking seriously the need to become educated about the history and traditions of other Christian communities? If not, how can we truly come to respect the differences that make them gifted by the Spirit? The challenge is to stretch out our hands in friendship and to collaborate in works of charity and love. Christians need to come together in prayer and to celebrate what makes us different as well as to celebrate what makes us one. Only as one community of Christians will we realize the full power of what it means to act in Christ, who is priest, prophet, and king.

❖ Discussion Questions ❖

1. What actions do you take personally to promote Christian unity?

2. How would you describe your parish's attitude toward relationships with non-Catholic Christians?

3. What common activities or opportunities for prayer do you see taking place between your parish and other Christian communities?

4. How might you envision the promotion of education on the history and theology of Christian communities in your local community?

5. Consider Congar's call for contrition. What steps do you think the Catholic Church needs to take to make amends for past failures to respect the baptismal identity of non-Catholic Christians?

ABOUT THE AUTHOR

✤

Stephen S. Wilbricht, a religious of the Congregation of Holy Cross, is an associate professor in the Department of Religious Studies and Theology at Stonehill College in Easton, Massachusetts. Prior to pursuing a doctorate in liturgical studies at the Catholic University of America in Washington, DC, he enjoyed seven years of pastoral ministry in two parishes in the Phoenix area. He has been a member of the North American Academy of Liturgy since 2011, participating in the work of the Christian Initiation Seminar. His major research interests revolve around the work of the liturgical movement and issues of present-day liturgical renewal. He is the author of *Rehearsing God's Just Kingdom: The Eucharistic Vision of Mark Searle* (Liturgical Press, 2013), *The Role of the Priest in Christian Initiation* (Liturgy Training Publications, 2017), and *Baptismal Ecclesiology and the "Order of Christian Funerals"* (Liturgy Training Publications, 2018).

ABOUT THE ARTIST

✤

James B. Janknegt lives and paints in Elgin, Texas. He has exhibited his paintings widely throughout Texas and in Washington, DC, and in the Museum of Biblical Art in New York. He has a bachelor of fine arts degree from the University of Texas at Austin and a master of arts degree and a master of fine arts degree from the University of Iowa in studio art. More of his work can be seen at www.bcartfarm.com.